MW01152749

From Egg to Snake

Following the Life Cycle

by
Suzanne Slade

illustrated by
Jeff Yesh

PICTURE WINDOW BOOKS
Minneapolis, Minnesota

Thanks to our advisers for their expertise, research, and advice:

John Krenz, Ph.D., Professor of Biology
Minnesota State University, Mankato

Terry Flaherty, Ph.D., Professor of English
Minnesota State University, Mankato

Editor: Shelly Lyons
Designer: Lori Bye
Page Production: Melissa Kes
Art Director: Nathan Gassman
Editorial Director: Nick Healy
The illustrations in this book were created digitally.

Picture Window Books
151 Good Counsel Drive
P.O. Box 669
Mankato, MN 56002-0669
877-845-8392
www.picturewindowbooks.com

Photo Credits: SuperStock/age fotostock, 23

All books published by Picture Window Books
are manufactured with paper containing at least
10 percent post-consumer waste.

Library of Congress Cataloging-in-Publication Data
Slade, Suzanne.
From egg to snake : following the life cycle / by Suzanne Slade ;
illustrated by Jeff Yesh.
p. cm. — (Amazing Science: Life cycle)
ISBN 978-1-4048-5153-5 (library binding)
1. Snakes—Life cycles—Juvenile literature. I. Yesh, Jeff, 1971- ill. II. Title.
QL666.06S47 2009
597.96'2—dc22   2008037901

Table of Contents

Amazing Snakes

Snakes are amazing animals that live in almost every part of the world. Although these long, thin creatures don't have legs, they can move with lightning speed.

Snakes come in many colors and sizes. A tiny thread snake is just 4.5 inches (11 centimeters) long, while some python snakes are more than 33 feet (10 meters) long. There are about 3,000 different kinds of snakes. This book shares the life cycle of a smooth green snake.

Smooth green snakes live in wet, grassy areas and forests. They are found in northeastern Canada and western parts of the United States. These bright green snakes have a white or yellow belly.

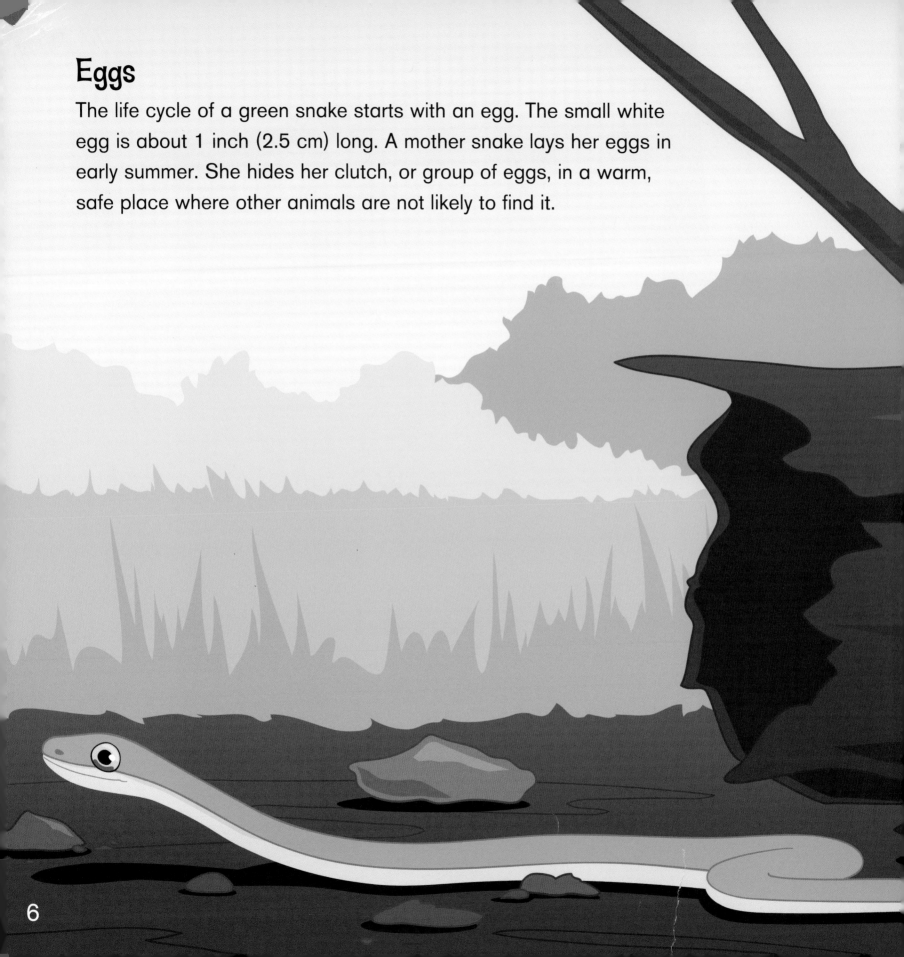

Eggs

The life cycle of a green snake starts with an egg. The small white egg is about 1 inch (2.5 cm) long. A mother snake lays her eggs in early summer. She hides her clutch, or group of eggs, in a warm, safe place where other animals are not likely to find it.

Most snakes do not stay with their eggs after laying them. The eggs are usually placed in a protected place. Sometimes they are buried or placed beneath rotting leaves.

Growing Inside

Inside the small eggs, new lives are beginning to form. These growing snakes are called embryos. An embryo gets its food from the yolk sac.

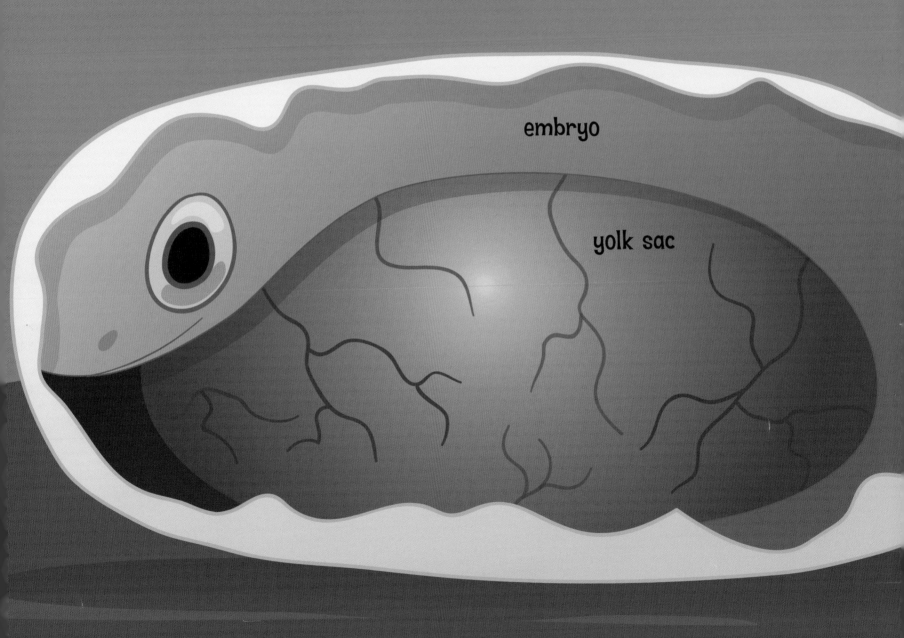

embryo

yolk sac

The eggshell is not hard like a bird's egg. It feels like leather. Tiny holes let in water and air for the growing embryo. The holes also allow a gas called carbon dioxide to leave the egg.

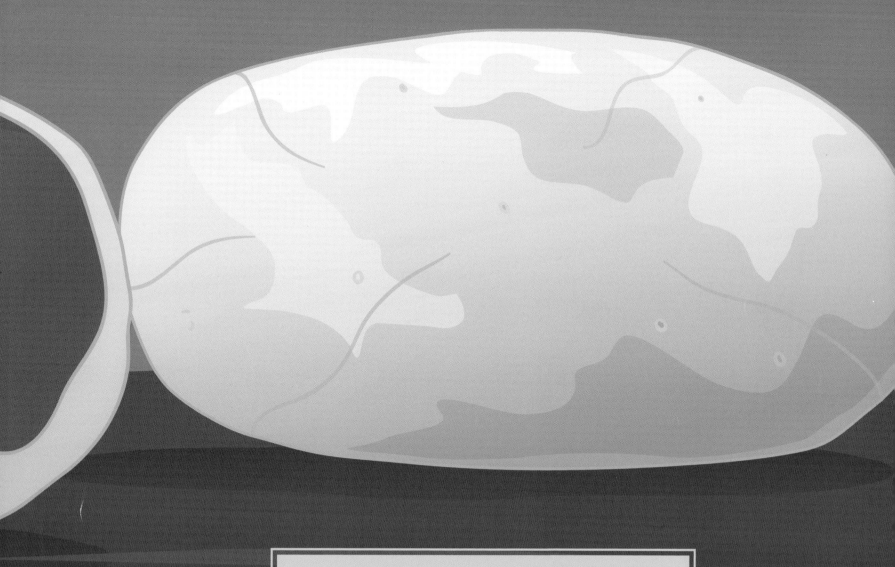

Most snakes lay eggs, but some give birth to live snakes. Snakes that lay eggs usually live in warm places. Snakes that give birth to live snakes are usually found in cooler areas or where egg predators are common.

Hatching Out

Green snakes usually hatch from their eggs within 30 days. A young snake is called a juvenile. It is about 3 to 5 inches (8 to 13 cm) long and has dark green skin.

Unhatched smooth green snakes have an egg tooth.
They use the sharp tooth to cut through the eggshell.
The tooth drops off soon after hatching.

On Its Own

Because its parents do not care for it, a juvenile snake is forced to take care of itself. This tiny hunter searches for small prey such as spiders and snails.

Green snakes hunt during the day. They use their excellent eyesight to spot insects moving in the grass.

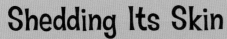

Shedding Its Skin

A juvenile snake grows very quickly, but its scaly skin does not. When a snake outgrows its skin, it sheds the outer layer, or covering. Beneath the shedding layer is a new layer of skin that fits just right. A snake sheds several times during its first year of life.

A snake may rub against something hard, such as a rock or tree trunk, to help its old skin start to shed. A green snake's skin gets brighter with each shedding.

15

Adulthood

A green snake becomes an adult when it is around 3 years old. When fully grown, it is about 12 to 22 inches (30 to 56 cm) long.

A hungry adult eats worms, caterpillars, crickets, grasshoppers, beetles, and other large insects. It stays safe from its enemies by hiding under green leaves and in tall grass.

A snake is covered with dry scales. The scales make up a tough outer layer. The layer protects the snake from sharp objects and biting insects. It helps keep water from leaving the snake's body. A snake also uses its scales to grip the ground, so it can move forward.

Time to Mate

At 3 years old, a smooth green snake is ready to find a mate. Mating usually happens during late summer. A snake uses its sense of smell to find the right partner.

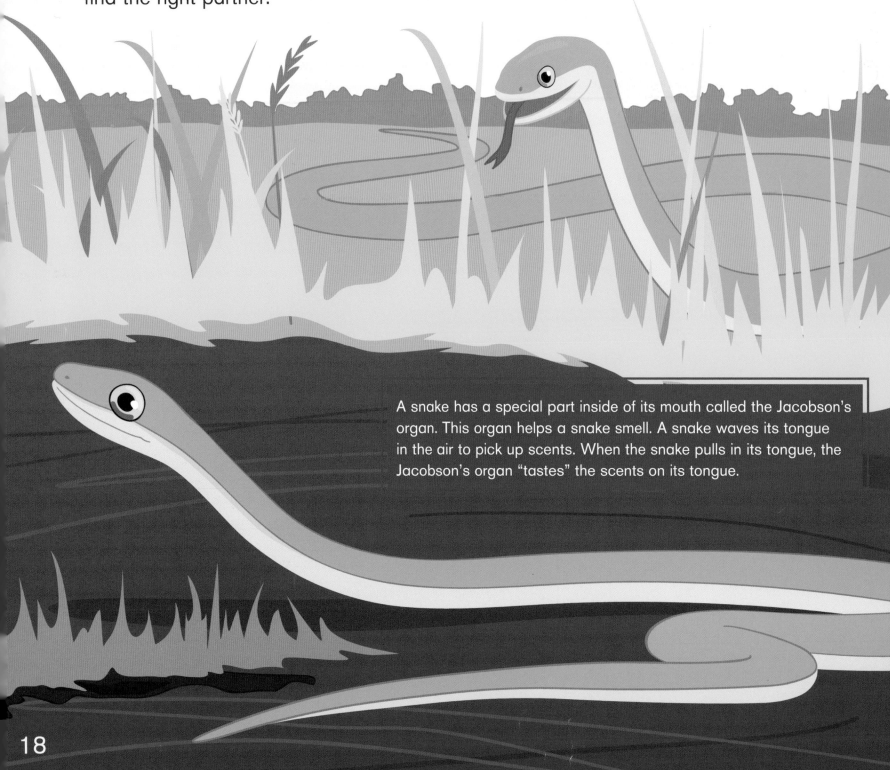

A snake has a special part inside of its mouth called the Jacobson's organ. This organ helps a snake smell. A snake waves its tongue in the air to pick up scents. When the snake pulls in its tongue, the Jacobson's organ "tastes" the scents on its tongue.

A green snake curls up underground and hibernates, or sleeps, during winter. When the weather warms in spring, the sleepy snake wakes up.

New Beginnings

About 10 to 11 months after mating, a female snake looks for a safe place to lay her eggs. She will lay about three to 12 eggs in a clutch. All of the eggs hatch at the same time. Each of these tiny snakes begins a new life cycle. A smooth green snake can live as long as six years.

Different types of snakes lay different-sized clutches. For example, an Indian snake can lay as many as 100 eggs. Other snakes lay only one or two eggs at a time.

21

Life Cycle of a Smooth Green Snake

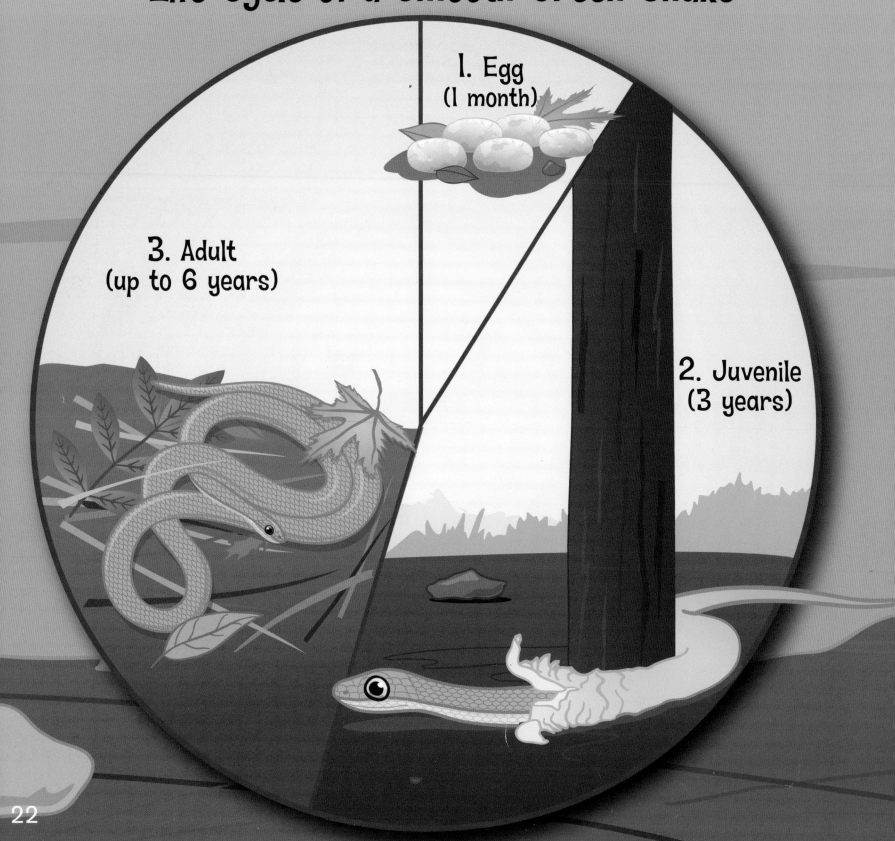

1. Egg
(1 month)

2. Juvenile
(3 years)

3. Adult
(up to 6 years)

Fun Facts

- A green snake has two colors, blue and yellow, inside of its skin. When a green snake dies, the yellow color in its skin disappears, but the blue does not. As a result, the dead snake turns blue.

- A snake is a cold-blooded animal. This means its body does not make heat. A snake will move to a warmer place, such as a sunny rock, if it is cold. When a snake gets too hot, it may slither into the shade or a cool spot underground.

- A snake does not have ears. It must put its lower jaw on the ground to hear. Tiny ground movements travel from a snake's jaw to its inner ear.

- About one-third of all snakes make a liquid poison called venom. Venomous snakes bite their prey and release venom through their teeth. Venom can seriously hurt, or even kill, animals.

- The Brahminy blind snake does not have to mate to produce young. This small, 6-inch (15-cm) long female snake can create new females all by herself.

Smooth green snake

Glossary

carbon dioxide—the air that people and animals breathe out

clutch—a group or nest of eggs

embryo—an animal that is just beginning to grow before birth or hatching

hatch—to break out of an egg

hibernate—to sleep deeply or rest quietly during winter

mate—to join together to produce young

predators—animals that hunt and eat other animals for food

prey—animals that are hunted by other animals for food

shed—to drop or fall off

yolk sac—a sack inside of an egg, full of food for the unhatched animal

To Learn More

More Books to Read

Crossingham, John, and Bobbie Kalman. *The Life Cycle of a Snake.* New York: Crabtree Pub. Co., 2003.

Mitchell, Melanie. *Snakes.* Minneapolis: Lerner Publications, 2003.

Watts, Barrie. *Snake.* North Mankato, Minn.: Smart Apple Media, 2002.

On the Web

FactHound offers a safe, fun way to find educator-approved Internet sites related to this book.

Here's what you do:
1. Visit *www.facthound.com*
2. Choose your grade level.
3. Begin your search.

This book's ID number is 9781404851535

Look for all of the books in the Amazing Science: Life Cycles series:

From Caterpillar to Butterfly: Following the Life Cycle
From Egg to Snake: Following the Life Cycle
From Mealworm to Beetle: Following the Life Cycle
From Pup to Rat: Following the Life Cycle
From Puppy to Dog: Following the Life Cycle
From Seed to Apple Tree: Following the Life Cycle
From Seed to Daisy: Following the Life Cycle
From Seed to Maple Tree: Following the Life Cycle
From Seed to Pine Tree: Following the Life Cycle
From Tadpole to Frog: Following the Life Cycle